MW01077445

$\mathcal{P}$ARENTING

Loving Our Children with God's Love

9 studies
for individuals or groups

Richard Patterson Jr.

With Notes for Leaders

IVP Connect

An imprint of InterVarsity Press
Downers Grove, Illinois

InterVarsity Press
P.O. Box 1400, Downers Grove, IL 60515-1426
World Wide Web: www.ivpress.com
E-mail: mail@ivpress.com

InterVarsity Press® is the book-publishing division of InterVarsity Christian Fellowship/USA®, a student movement active on campus at hundreds of universities, colleges and schools of nursing in the United States of America, and a member movement of the International Fellowship of Evangelical Students. For information about local and regional activities, write Public Relations Dept., InterVarsity Christian Fellowship/USA, 6400 Schroeder Rd., P.O. Box 7895, Madison, WI 53707-7895, or visit the IVCF website at <www.intervarsity.org>.

Cover image: Klaus Nigge/National Geographic Image Collection

ISBN-10: 0-8308-3131-2
ISBN-13: 978-0-8308-3131-9

Printed in the United States of America ∞

P	18	17	16	15	14	13	12	11	10	9	8	7	6	5	4	3	2	1
Y	20	19	18	17	16	15	14	13	12	11	10	09	08	07	06				

Contents

Getting the Most Out of *Parenting*

Being a parent today is a lot like running a marathon. It requires a major amount of discipline and endurance. Technology—computers, video games and even television—opens a complex, seductive and sometimes threatening world to young children. Conflicting and changing moral values confront and confuse adolescents. Fluctuating social norms and family forms can even make parents unsure of what is true and reliable. These challenges add to the normal anxieties of most parents as they search for sure and trustworthy principles to help them be the good parents they want to be. And Christian parents, who want to raise children who will share their faith, carry additional hopes and dreams.

Our natural tendency is to turn to experts. That can be a good thing, and there are plenty of them out there eager to offer advice. But as a parent for over thirty years, I've learned that God has given us plenty of time-tested, reliable advice and guidelines already. They've been fully tested by parents over the centuries, and any parent can rely on them. After all, God is the "expert of experts."

This guide will take you through nine studies designed to uncover some of the major parenting insights found in the Bible—basic insights and guidelines on which you can base your day-to-day parenting decisions and practices. Each study covers a basic challenge of parenting. The Bible passage chosen for study may not always be the most common or expected one but is intended to stimulate thinking and discussion from perhaps a new or fresh perspective. The "Now or Later" sections offer you opportunities to begin to apply the principles discussed in the study in immediate, practical ways.

Parenting today is surely a challenge, a heavy responsibility. But it is also a great privilege and a great joy! The Bible says that children are a reward from God and a rich blessing (Psalm 127:3, 5). May they truly be so for you.

Suggestions for Individual Study

1. As you begin each study, pray that God will speak to you through his Word.

2. Read the introduction to the study and respond to the personal reflection question or exercise. This is designed to help you focus on God and on the theme of the study.

3. Each study deals with a particular passage—so that you can delve into the author's meaning in that context. Read and reread the passage to be studied. The questions are written using the language of the New International Version, so you may wish to use that version of the Bible. The New Revised Standard Version is also recommended.

4. This is an inductive Bible study, designed to help you discover for yourself what Scripture is saying. The study includes three types of questions. *Observation* questions ask about the basic facts: who, what, when, where and how. *Interpretation* questions delve into the meaning of the passage. *Application* questions help you discover the implications of the text for growing in Christ. These three keys unlock the treasures of Scripture.

Write your answers to the questions in the spaces provided or in a personal journal. Writing can bring clarity and deeper understanding of yourself and of God's Word.

5. It might be good to have a Bible dictionary handy. Use it to look up any unfamiliar words, names or places.

6. Use the prayer suggestion to guide you in thanking God for what you have learned and to pray about the applications that have come to mind.

7. You may want to go on to the suggestion under "Now or Later," or you may want to use that idea for your next study.

Suggestions for Members of a Group Study

1. Come to the study prepared. Follow the suggestions for individual study mentioned above. You will find that careful preparation will greatly enrich your time spent in group discussion.

2. Be willing to participate in the discussion. The leader of your group will not be lecturing. Instead, he or she will be encouraging the members of the group to discuss what they have learned. The leader will be asking the questions that are found in this guide.

3. Stick to the topic being discussed. Your answers should be based on the verses which are the focus of the discussion and not on outside authorities such as commentaries or speakers. These studies focus on a particular passage of Scripture. Only rarely should you refer to other portions of the Bible. This allows for everyone to participate in in-depth study on equal ground.

4. Be sensitive to the other members of the group. Listen attentively when they describe what they have learned. You may be surprised by their insights! Each question assumes a variety of answers. Many questions do not have "right" answers, particularly questions that aim at meaning or application. Instead the questions push us to explore the passage more thoroughly.

When possible, link what you say to the comments of others. Also, be affirming whenever you can. This will encourage some of the more hesitant members of the group to participate.

5. Be careful not to dominate the discussion. We are sometimes so eager to express our thoughts that we leave too little opportunity for others to respond. By all means participate! But allow others to also.

6. Expect God to teach you through the passage being discussed and through the other members of the group. Pray that you will have an enjoyable and profitable time together, but also that as a result of the study you will find ways that you can take action individually and/or as a group.

7. Remember that anything said in the group is considered confidential and should not be discussed outside the group unless specific permission is given to do so.

8. If you are the group leader, you will find additional suggestions at the back of the guide.

1

A "God's-Eye View" of Our Children

Mark 10:13-16

There was a time, a generation or two ago, when children were to be "seen and not heard." They were seen as mostly "potential" and supposed to listen and learn from adults. Perhaps we see our children somewhat differently today, but what does the Lord see when he looks on our children? Does he see just "potential adults," "vessels to be filled" or something more? Do our children have anything significant to teach *us*? In the busyness and stress of daily family life, it's easy to lose sight of just how precious and special our children are—or should be—and why. Let's get a "God's-eye view" of children from this passage in Mark's gospel.

GROUP DISCUSSION. If someone were to ask you what "value" your children are to you, what would you say? Think of some children (your own or someone else's) that you admire. Why is that so? What makes children "valuable"?

PERSONAL REFLECTION. Reflect on how you feel you were regarded by the important adults in your life when you were a child. Thank God for those who valued you and made you feel valued. Thank God for your own children and reflect on the ways your daily interactions with them reflect your love for them and the value you see in them.

In this brief passage, and similar passages in Matthew 19:13-15 and Luke 18:15-17, we get a rare glimpse of Jesus interacting with children and see just how special they are to him and why. Jesus had been teaching the crowds, first answering the Pharisees' questions about divorce and then answering the disciples' questions about his response. *Read Mark 10:13-16.*

---

1. In light of this passage, how would you describe Jesus' attitude toward children?

---

2. How would you say the Lord's attitude toward children differs from the general attitude of our society toward children today?

---

3. How do you think the disciples' actions and attitudes made the children feel?

How might they have shaped the children's attitudes toward Jesus?

4. What makes your children special to you?

5. What would you have done (and felt) if you had been a parent of one of those children "rebuked" by Jesus' disciples?

6. Why do you think the disciples rebuked the parents who wanted to bring their children to Jesus?

7. How do adult Christians (other than parents) sometimes "hinder" children from coming to Jesus today?

What are some ways parents may (even unintentionally) hinder their children from coming to Jesus?

8. How does a child "receive the kingdom" of God?

What might that teach you about receiving it yourself?

9. What do you think are the most important ways that parents can reflect to their children the attitude Jesus has toward them?

10. Jesus had an urgent mission to adults and had many demands on him, yet he made it a priority to take time to hug and bless these children. How do you show your children that they are such a high priority to you?

11. Reflect specifically on your child's faith and character. What would you say you could learn from your children?

Pray that God helps you to show your children the same love, value and dignity in which he holds them.

Now or Later

Recall how your actions this week reflected (or didn't) a "God's-eye view" of your children. What are some specific ways you can more clearly see your children through God's eyes? Look for ways to treat them accordingly.

What are some ways you can "let [your] children come" to Jesus this week and not hinder them?

2

A Firm Family Foundation

A number of studies in recent years have revealed the characteristics of strong, happy marriages and also shown the negative effects of divorce on children. God has made marriage the context for sexual intimacy and for raising children. Although divorced and single parents also raise happy, well-adjusted children, God's purpose is that children be raised in a family built on a lasting marriage that is sustained and nurtured by faith. That's the ideal, but it takes real commitment and sustained effort to make it happen. And the "keys" to a strong, lasting marriage aren't always obvious.

GROUP DISCUSSION. Think of some marriages you know of that seem strong and happy. What makes them that way?

What impact do you think these marriages have on the children involved? Why?

PERSONAL REFLECTION. Reflect on your parents' marriage. Thank God for all the good that came to you as a result. If it was an unhappy or broken marriage, reflect on why that was the case and ask God to help you not repeat unhealthy patterns in your own marriage.

As every parent knows, parenting is hard work and is much easier when shared by a loving partner! This passage isn't specifically about marriage but has some important insights for marriage partners. *Read Ecclesiastes 4:9-12.*

1. What are some reasons given in this passage that "two are better than one"?

2. What do you think the writer means by "a cord of three strands"?

3. What would you say are the most significant advantages of two rather than one in parenting?

4. Why is a strong marriage so important to children?

5. What are some ways that "one falls down" as a parent?

How do (or could) you and your spouse help each other in those situations?

_____

6. What kind of relationship would you say the "two" in this passage have?

_____

7. How important would you say a common faith is to spouses? Why?

_____

8. Do you think it's important that your spouse also be your close (or closest) friend? Why or why not?

_____

9. What factors or influences threaten to overpower (v. 12) marriage partners today?

How can spouses help defend each other against these factors?

_____

10. Loyalty is important in any close relationship (v. 12). How can and should spouses show loyalty to each other in daily life both inside and outside the family?

---

11. Using the principles in this passage, what are the two or three most important pieces of advice you'd give an engaged couple who wants to build a strong marriage?

---

12. In what ways can you strengthen your own marriage relationship using insights from this passage?

Pray for God's help to have a strong marriage that will be a gift both to you and your children.

Now or Later

Read 1 Corinthians 7:1-16 and Ephesians 5:21-33. Think of some ways that you and your spouse strengthened (or weakened) your relationship this week. What lessons did you learn that you can apply in the week ahead? Were you loyal and a good friend to your spouse?

Look for one or two specific ways this week to grow together as a couple and to demonstrate to your children what a strong, happy marriage looks like. Assure them that you will always be a couple committed to each other and to them—that you'll always be a family.

3

Demostrating
God's Love

I've heard it said, "Children grow up to be the love they've known." If that's true, then the kind of love we experience as a child powerfully shapes the adult we become. Surely, that love also influences the extent to which we are able to love ourselves and others. Loving our children, then, is no little thing! But don't all parents love their children? Yes, in some sense, all probably do. But all "loves" are not necessarily equal. How can we leave our children no doubt that they are loved? How can we love them with true, godly love?

GROUP DISCUSSION. Think of some parents you admire. What do you think is the most important or striking way they show love to their children?

What effect can you see that it has on their children?

What makes children doubt their parents' love?

PERSONAL REFLECTION. Reflect on the ways God has shown you his love. Thank him for his love for you, especially as you experienced it through your parents. Thank him for the privilege of showing his love to your children and reflect on the challenges and joys of that.

In this study we look at a well-known passage through the lens of the parent-child relationship. *Read 1 Corinthians 13:1-8.*

1. What are some of the characteristics of genuine love that Paul gives here?

2. Which of the characteristics of love given here would you say most parents you know are strongest and weakest in?

3. In what ways, if any, did your parents' love reflect the love described above?

In what ways did their love fall short?

How did their love shape the person you've become (for good or ill) and the way you relate to God?

4. Why would Paul say that love is such an important factor in all we do or are?

---

5. Dealing with needy, noisy and unruly children can be overwhelming for any parent at times. In those situations, how is it possible to love children with a love that is patient, kind and not easily angered (vv. 4-5)?

---

6. How might this description of godly love affect the way a parent disciplines a child?

---

7. How can a parent hold a child accountable for repeated misdeeds while "keeping no record of wrongs" (v. 5)?

---

8. What are some things a parent's love has to "trust," "hope" or "persevere" in?

---

9. "Love never fails" (v. 8). What are some situations that might stretch your love for your child to the breaking point?

How might this passage help you in such a situation?

10. Our society conceives of love in ways that would seem foreign to Paul. How does his concept of love differ from that of many parents today?

11. What could you do to grow in your own understanding and expression of godly love?

12. In what specific ways could you apply the kind of love described in this passage to your parenting?

Thank God for his gracious and sacrificial love for you. Pray for God's help to show your children that same love.

Now or Later

Recall any ways that the love you showed your children this week fell short of God's love for them. What are two or three specific ways you can show them God's love more clearly in the future?

Look for ways this week to show your children love that is patient the way God is patient with you. How can you hold them accountable for wrongdoing without always "keeping a record of wrongs"? Are there specific ways you can show them kindness? When anger and resentment threaten, how can your spouse help?

4

Training Our Children in God's Ways

Deuteronomy 6:1-9

Ours is a society that seems to want to do everything quickly and easily. But there aren't any shortcuts or quick and easy ways to nurture faith in our children. Yet, the Bible assigns parents that responsibility. However, God never gives us a task without providing all that we need to know to carry it out. Through Moses, God gave us some useful tools and principles that parents can use to guide them as they strive to pass on their faith to their children in the midst of their busy, complicated lives. In this study, we'll see if we can discover some of those "tools."

GROUP DISCUSSION. If you were advising a newly married couple how to prepare to nurture faith in their children, what would you tell them?

PERSONAL REFLECTION. Reflect on the awesome privilege and responsibility you have as a parent in nurturing the faith of your children. What is exciting to you when you think about this? What is intimidating or overwhelming?

Our jobs, church and family life all put heavy demands on our time. Here, Moses provides parents some practical and effective guidelines for nurturing faith in our children. *Read Deuteronomy 6:1-9.*

---

1. Verse 1 sets out Moses' purpose in teaching Israel. Verses 2-3 set out our purpose in learning God's ways. What is our goal?

---

2. How would you describe the method Moses tells Israelite parents to use in training their children in God's ways?

---

3. What are some ways that your parents and parents you know attempt to pass on their faith to their children?

What ways would you say are most or least effective?

---

4. Why do you think it is important that God's Word be in a parent's heart in order to be able to train a child in godly living?

---

5. Why do you think Moses doesn't stress regularly reading the Bible together?

6. What do you think it means to "impress" God's commandments on your children (v. 7)?

7. Daily family life is full of pressures, distractions and chores.
How can a parent be alert to opportunities to impress God's
Word on their child's heart?

How do you keep alert?

8. Given what you see in this passage, what opportunities does
your daily family life provide for nurturing your children's
faith?

9. How does your daily family life reflect to your children your
own personal love and respect for God's Word and ways?

10. How might Christian art and music build your child's faith?

How do (or might) they do so in your home?

11. In light of this passage, what role in nurturing your child's faith would you assign to Sunday school and similar formal religious education experiences?

What part, if any, do you expect other Christians to play in training your children in Christian living?

12. In what specific ways can you have God's ways "upon your heart" so you can better impress them on your children (vv. 6-7)?

Pray for God to help you have his Word in your heart and communicate it clearly to your children. Confess where your attitude and practice before your children has fallen short.

Now or Later

Recall some times this past week when your family life offered opportunities to teach your children God's Word and ways. How did you use them? How could you have used them better? How can you and your spouse help each other be alert to these opportunities?

What can you do to impress God's Word and ways on your children this week? How will you deepen your own relationship with God? Make a list of some specific things you'll ask God to help you do and be in the week ahead.

5

The Seasons
of Parenting

Ecclesiastes 3:1-8

If you ask a parent what are the top three stressors he or she faces, one of them is sure to be time pressures. How can your child attend the after-school soccer practice and still be home for dinner? Why did the company have to schedule that last-minute meeting on Saturday? Although we all have the same 1,440 minutes in each day, there never seems to be enough time to do the really important things, such as just being together, having fun and enjoying each other as a family. Parents are stewards of the family's time, just as with its other resources. Is there a way to slow down in this sped-up age? Maybe understanding something of the seasons of parenting will help us set priorities and find a proper time for everything.

GROUP DISCUSSION. What are some of the ways that time pressures affect your family?

Why do you think this is so?

PERSONAL REFLECTION. Reflect on the simple joys that you

experience in your family in the midst of your busy lives. Thank God for them.

Let's slow down for a few minutes and take another look at time and parenting from God's perspective. *Read Ecclesiastes 3:1-8.*

---

1. The language of this text is very emotive. What are your thoughts and feelings as you read through it?

---

2. The passage begins with the statement, "There is a time for everything." How does the rest of the text support that statement?

---

3. Read through the passage again with family in mind. What specific family activities does the writer here assure you there is a proper time and season for?

---

4. What important activities does your family find are most often squeezed out in the press of busy daily life?

---

5. How does your family take "time to laugh" and "dance"— regularly taking time to have fun together?

How do such fun times contribute to your family's health?

6. Parenting is an activity that has stages or seasons as children grow. What season(s) would you say you are in (or have gone through) as a parent?

7. What particular dreams, goals or priorities attach to your current parenting season?

8. What dreams, goals or priorities might be postponed (in a "time to give up") to a later season?

9. What is an example of an important "time to be silent" for a parent?

10. Which of the times and seasons listed in this passage would you say are most vital to a happy, healthy family life and why?

11. Ultimately this passage reinforces the truth that God is in control in all of the seasons of life. How does knowing this contribute to your family life and your parenting experience?

Pray for a healthy sense of the needs of your family's particular season and how you are spending your time together.

Now or Later

Reflect again on your current parenting season. What are two or three of the most important goals or priorities you and your spouse share for this season? What will you do this week to begin or continue to realize these goals?

In light of the time pressures on your family life, what priorities might need to change during this season? What fun or rewarding activities might you begin (or plan) this week?

6

Godly Discipline in the Home

Life is exhausting—and that can affect how we practice discipline in our families. Some days, for example, we may let a child's rudeness pass for the sake of our peaceful dinner, or just to avoid a fight, we may pick up a few toys rather than calling our kids back to do it themselves.

We often think of discipline as a negative thing—a "necessary evil" or punishment—but from God's perspective, discipline is really a very positive thing. After all, the word *discipline* comes from the same root as "disciple." Giving godly discipline is part of our calling as parents. In this study, we'll try to discover just what godly discipline might look like.

GROUP DISCUSSION. Do you think good discipline is harder to achieve today than in previous generations? Why or why not?

PERSONAL REFLECTION. Reflect on how your parents disciplined you—the good and the bad ways. Ask God to show you how to discipline your children in a way that best reflects his love and desires for them.

It just makes sense that the way you understand discipline affects the goals you have for it, how you carry it out and what it ultimately achieves. *Read Hebrews 12:5-11.*

1. This text may seem harsh. How do you respond to this passage?

2. How would you compare the way God disciplines us to the way we should discipline our children in our role as parents?

3. There may be any number of reasons for disciplining a child, but what would you say should be the overall purpose of parental discipline?

4. What were some of the ways that discipline was handled when you were a child?

How do they measure up to what you've found in this passage?

5. In light of Paul's description of discipline, would you say discipline has to "hurt" in some way to be effective?

6. If it's true that discipline is often seen in a negative light, how might this passage help change that?

---

7. What methods of discipline, if any, would Paul say should be off-limits in a Christian home?

Which are most desirable?

---

8. How can parental discipline encourage a child?

---

9. What kind of discipline produces respect in the one being disciplined (v. 9)?

---

10. From verses 10-11 how would you describe God's ultimate goal in disciplining us?

---

11. What principles or guidelines of godly discipline do you see in this passage?

12. How has this passage changed or broadened your understanding of Christian parental discipline?

_____

13. How can you discipline your children in such a way as to
also be discipling them?

*Ask God to help you reflect his loving discipling of you when you're
disciplining your children.*

Now or Later

Think of some situations where you disciplined your child this
week. What did you do that was in accordance with Paul's
counsel? What might you have done differently?

How will you disciple your children through your discipline
this week?

Think of two or three specific goals for your parental discipline
in the week ahead. Perhaps take time to explain to your children the loving reasons for your discipline and your goals for
them. What changes in your attitudes or methods will you
make?

7

God Through Our Children's Eyes

Psalm 145

Child development specialists tell us that children form their earliest impressions of God from their interactions with their parents. That can be pretty frightening! In a real sense, our children get to know God through knowing us. We're the lens through which they first "see" him. If that's true, we want to be sure we have a close relationship with our heavenly "parent" and know God as well as possible, so we can accurately reflect to our children who God really is and what he is like.

GROUP DISCUSSION. What images of God do you have in your heart and mind? Are some good and others not? Where did they come from?

How might your images of God shape the way you parent and the impressions of God you give your children?

PERSONAL REFLECTION. Reflect on the ways that your parents communicated (or may have miscommunicated) anything of the character of God to you. Thank God for any way they helped you come to know and respond to his love. Think about what it is about God that you want to communicate to your children.

How does our parenting relationship with our children reflect the way God parents us? What does it say to them about who God is? Let's see what we can discover. *Read Psalm 145.*

1. What characteristics of God do you find in this passage?

2. Verse 4 says, "One generation will commend your works to another." What specific things will be celebrated (vv. 4-7)?

3. In what ways might God be acting similarly to a parent in this passage?

4. Study verses 8-9. How have you recently experienced God's goodness?

5. God receives great praise from the psalmist for his goodness toward us. Should parents expect their children to always love and appreciate them? Why or why not?

6. How has your relationship with God shaped your own view of what a parent is and does?

7. Compassion is mentioned twice in describing God (vv. 8-9). Is it possible to be truly compassionate and still be firm in setting limits and maintaining discipline? If so, how?

8. Verse 19 says that God "fulfills the desires of those who fear him." To what extent and on what basis do good parents "fulfill the desires" of their children?

9. Which of these characteristics of God as parent are hardest for you to emulate and why?

10. What characteristics of God would you say that you most accurately reflect to your children?

11. What do you hope that your children will learn about God as a result of your parenting and their relationship with you?

12. How might you change your parenting to more closely reflect the nature of God to your children?

Pray that you will grow in your own relationship with God and be more fully able to reflect his character to your children.

Now or Later

Reflect again on your relationship with God and the image of him you carry. How has that image shaped who you are as a person and a parent? Does your image of God need to be changed in any way?

What are at least two areas in which you could more accurately reflect God's character in your parenting? In what specific ways could you begin to do that in the week ahead? How can you grow in your own relationship with God this week?

8

Coping with the "Lost" Child

Luke 15:11-32

A "lost" (or "prodigal") child is often the cause of anguished questions and searing heartbreak. "What did I do wrong?" a parent asks. "Why did my child reject all that we taught her?" There are few answers but many opportunities for sadness and for carrying a heavy burden of guilt (such as when other folks' children attend church regularly or go off on mission trips while ours is noticeably absent!). Is there reason for hope? What can such a parent do?

GROUP DISCUSSION. Think of some lost or prodigal children you know or have known (perhaps including yourself). What might have led them (or you) to that choice?

Do you know some parents coping with such a situation? How do they do it?

PERSONAL REFLECTION. Reflect on how you would react if you were a parent of a lost child. Would you be able to hope for their "return"? Thank God for his unconditional love for you and all lost children.

In this well-known parable of the lost son (commonly known as the "Prodigal Son"), there is hope for every parent of a "lost" child. The child may be lost now, but God isn't finished yet. *Read Luke 15:11-32.*

1. What do you think led the younger son to leave?

2. What attitude does it seem that the father had throughout this ordeal?

3. How would you have felt if you had been that father?

4. What kinds of behaviors would lead you to consider a child of yours as lost?

5. What would you likely be doing while your child was lost?

6. How would you characterize this father's love for his son?

_____

7. Why do you think the older brother couldn't share in his father's joy?

_____

8. Could you receive back a lost but repentant child in the same spirit as this father? Why or why not?

_____

9. What attitudes exhibited by father and younger son permitted the successful return of the lost son to the family?

_____

10. What conditions would you set on any such return?

_____

11. What can a parent do to try to prevent their child from becoming a lost child?

12. What responsibility do Christian parents bear when their children are lost?

---

13. If you had a lost child, how could you maintain hope in their return?

---

14. If you had a lost child, how would you answer someone who asked how your child "turned out"?

Pray that God will plant a deep, unshakeable love for him in the hearts of your children and that they may know both his unconditional love and yours.

Now or Later

Think of some families coping with a lost child. How could you encourage them? If your family is in that situation, what can you do this week to maintain hope and a compassionate, loving attitude toward your lost child?

What are some ways you can communicate unconditional love for your children this week? How can you make sure they know you are always ready to "take them back" with joy?

9

Creating a Legacy for Our Children

Joshua 4:1-9, 19-24

What's a legacy? What can we leave behind for our children? "Legacy" may most often bring to mind money. But as helpful as money can be to our children, a spiritual legacy is an even more valuable gift. It can be a living, enduring reminder and encouragement to our children of the faith that guided us, their parents. And it can guide them, too, long after we are gone. However, leaving a spiritual legacy isn't easy.

GROUP DISCUSSION. Think of some children you know that received legacies of different sorts from their parents. What were these legacies, and what impact did they have, for good or harm?

Consider the spiritual legacy you received from your parents. How has it helped or hindered your life?

PERSONAL REFLECTION. Reflect on any spiritual legacy you received from your parents. Thank God for the way it shaped your life for good. Pray for healing in regard to any negative areas.

Leaving a positive spiritual legacy to your children first requires knowing why and how to create it. Joshua knew—and did it. We can learn from Joshua how to do the same. We enter the story right after Israel crossed over the Jordan River into the Promised Land. They crossed while the river was at its spring flood stage, but God provided dry ground while they were crossing. God did a miracle for his people here, not unlike the crossing of the Red Sea on the flight from slavery in Egypt. *Read Joshua 4:1-9, 19-24.*

1. What does Joshua ask the people to do in verses 1-5?

2. What would be the message or legacy of the stones?

3. Why do you think Joshua chose a pile of stones as a means of commemorating God's help instead a making a written account?

4. Bring to mind a significant way God has worked in your life. How could you commemorate that in some way?

5. How was this memorial intended to impact the faith of future generations (vv. 21-24)?

_____

6. What kind of "stones" can parents today use to create a spiritual legacy for their children?

_____

7. How would you describe the kind of legacy you want to leave your children?

_____

8. What signs of God's goodness, faithfulness and activity in their lives do you want your children never to forget?

_____

9. How can you build those into their legacy?

_____

10. What is the hardest part for you of building a spiritual legacy for your children?

What can you do about it?

---

11. If you were asked the single most important thing parents can do to leave a spiritual legacy for their children, what would you say?

Pray that God will enable you to create a rich and lasting spiritual legacy for your children, stone by stone each day.

Now or Later

Think about how you have been creating (or neglecting to create) a spiritual legacy for your children this week. How intentional have you been? What "stones" are available for your use?

What are some specific steps that you can take this week to begin or continue creating a spiritual legacy for your children? How can you and your spouse work together on this most effectively? What will you do to strengthen any of your areas of weakness?

Leader's Notes

Leading a Bible discussion can be an enjoyable and rewarding experience. But it can also be *scary*—especially if you've never done it before. If this is your feeling, you're in good company. When God asked Moses to lead the Israelites out of Egypt, he replied, "O LORD, please send someone else to do it" (Ex 4:13). It was the same with Solomon, Jeremiah and Timothy, but God helped these people in spite of their weaknesses, and he will help you as well.

You don't need to be an expert on the Bible or a trained teacher to lead a Bible discussion. The idea behind these inductive studies is that the leader guides group members to discover for themselves what the Bible has to say. This method of learning will allow group members to remember much more of what is said than a lecture would.

These studies are designed to be led easily. As a matter of fact, the flow of questions through the passage from observation to interpretation to application is so natural that you may feel that the studies lead themselves. This study guide is also flexible. You can use it with a variety of groups—student, professional, neighborhood or church groups. Each study takes forty-five to sixty minutes in a group setting.

There are some important facts to know about group dynamics and encouraging discussion. The suggestions listed below should enable you to effectively and enjoyably fulfill your role as leader.

Preparing for the Study

1. Ask God to help you understand and apply the passage in your own life. Unless this happens, you will not be prepared to lead others. Pray too for the various members of the group. Ask God to open your hearts to the message of his Word and motivate you to action.

2. Read the introduction to the entire guide to get an overview of the entire book and the issues which will be explored.

3. As you begin each study, read and reread the assigned Bible passage to familiarize yourself with it.

4. This study guide is based on the New International Version of the Bible. It will help you and the group if you use this translation as the basis for your study and discussion.

5. Carefully work through each question in the study. Spend time in meditation and reflection as you consider how to respond.

6. Write your thoughts and responses in the space provided in the study guide. This will help you to express your understanding of the passage clearly.

7. It might help to have a Bible dictionary handy. Use it to look up any unfamiliar words, names or places. (For additional help on how to study a passage, see chapter five of *How to Lead a LifeGuide Bible Study,* InterVarsity Press.)

8. Consider how you can apply the Scripture to your life. Remember that the group will follow your lead in responding to the studies. They will not go any deeper than you do.

9. Once you have finished your own study of the passage, familiarize yourself with the leader's notes for the study you are leading. These are designed to help you in several ways. First, they tell you the purpose the study guide author had in mind when writing the study. Take time to think through how the study questions work together to accomplish that purpose. Second, the notes provide you with additional background information or suggestions on group dynamics for various questions. This information can be useful when people have difficulty understanding or answering a question. Third, the leader's notes can alert you to potential problems you may encounter during the study.

10. If you wish to remind yourself of anything mentioned in the leader's notes, make a note to yourself below that question in the study.

Leading the Study

1. Begin the study on time. Open with prayer, asking God to help the group to understand and apply the passage.

2. Be sure that everyone in your group has a study guide. Encourage the group to prepare beforehand for each discussion by reading the introduction to the guide and by working through the questions in the study.

3. At the beginning of your first time together, explain that these studies are meant to be discussions, not lectures. Encourage the members of the group to participate. However, do not put pressure on those who may be hesitant to speak during the first few sessions. You may want to suggest the following guidelines to your group.

☐ Stick to the topic being discussed.

☐ Your responses should be based on the verses which are the focus of the discussion and not on outside authorities such as commentaries or speakers.

☐ These studies focus on a particular passage of Scripture. Only rarely should you refer to other portions of the Bible. This allows for everyone to participate in in-depth study on equal ground.

☐ Anything said in the group is considered confidential and will not be discussed outside the group unless specific permission is given to do so.

☐ We will listen attentively to each other and provide time for each person present to talk.

☐ We will pray for each other.

4. Have a group member read the introduction at the beginning of the discussion.

5. Every session begins with a group discussion question. The question or activity is meant to be used before the passage is read. The question introduces the theme of the study and encourages group members to begin to open up. Encourage as many members as possible to participate, and be ready to get the discussion going with your own response.

This section is designed to reveal where our thoughts or feelings need to be transformed by Scripture. That is why it is especially important not to read the passage before the discussion question is asked. The passage will tend to color the honest reactions people would otherwise give because they are, of course, supposed to think the way the Bible does.

You may want to supplement the group discussion question with an icebreaker to help people to get comfortable. See the community section of *Small Group Idea Book* for more ideas.

You also might want to use the personal reflection question with your group. Either allow a time of silence for people to respond individually or discuss it together.

6. Have a group member (or members if the passage is long) read aloud the passage to be studied. Then give people several minutes to read the passage again silently so that they can take it all in.

7. Question 1 will generally be an overview question designed to briefly survey the passage. Encourage the group to look at the whole passage, but try to avoid getting sidetracked by questions or issues that will be addressed later in the study.

8. As you ask the questions, keep in mind that they are designed to be used just as they are written. You may simply read them aloud. Or you may prefer to express them in your own words.

There may be times when it is appropriate to deviate from the study guide.

For example, a question may have already been answered. If so, move on to the next question. Or someone may raise an important question not covered in the guide. Take time to discuss it, but try to keep the group from going off on tangents.

9. Avoid answering your own questions. If necessary, repeat or rephrase them until they are clearly understood. Or point out something you read in the leader's notes to clarify the context or meaning. An eager group quickly becomes passive and silent if they think the leader will do most of the talking.

10. Don't be afraid of silence. People may need time to think about the question before formulating their answers.

11. Don't be content with just one answer. Ask, "What do the rest of you think?" or "Anything else?" until several people have given answers to the question.

12. Acknowledge all contributions. Try to be affirming whenever possible. Never reject an answer. If it is clearly off-base, ask, "Which verse led you to that conclusion?" or again, "What do the rest of you think?"

13. Don't expect every answer to be addressed to you, even though this will probably happen at first. As group members become more at ease, they will begin to truly interact with each other. This is one sign of healthy discussion.

14. Don't be afraid of controversy. It can be very stimulating. If you don't resolve an issue completely, don't be frustrated. Move on and keep it in mind for later. A subsequent study may solve the problem.

15. Periodically summarize what the group has said about the passage. This helps to draw together the various ideas mentioned and gives continuity to the study. But don't preach.

16. At the end of the Bible discussion you may want to allow group members a time of quiet to work on an idea under "Now or Later." Then discuss what you experienced. Or you may want to encourage group members to work on these ideas between meetings. Give an opportunity during the session for people to talk about what they are learning.

17. Conclude your time together with conversational prayer, adapting the prayer suggestion at the end of the study to your group. Ask for God's help in following through on the commitments you've made.

18. End on time.

Many more suggestions and helps are found in *How to Lead a LifeGuide Bible Study*.

Components of Small Groups
A healthy small group should do more than study the Bible. There are four

components to consider as you structure your time together.

Nurture. Small groups help us to grow in our knowledge and love of God. Bible study is the key to making this happen and is the foundation of your small group.

Community. Small groups are a great place to develop deep friendships with other Christians. Allow time for informal interaction before and after each study. Plan activities and games that will help you get to know each other. Spend time having fun together—going on a picnic or cooking dinner together.

Worship and prayer. Your study will be enhanced by spending time praising God together in prayer or song. Pray for each other's needs—and keep track of how God is answering prayer in your group. Ask God to help you to apply what you are learning in your study.

Outreach. Reaching out to others can be a practical way of applying what you are learning, and it will keep your group from becoming self-focused. Host a series of evangelistic discussions for your friends or neighbors. Clean up the yard of an elderly friend. Serve at a soup kitchen together, or spend a day working on a Habitat house.

Many more suggestions and helps in each of these areas are found in *Small Group Idea Book*. Information on building a small group can be found in *Small Group Leaders' Handbook* and *The Big Book on Small Groups* (both from Inter-Varsity Press). Reading through one of these books would be worth your time.

Study 1. A "God's-Eye View" of Our Children. Mark 10:13-16.
Purpose: To discover the high value that Jesus places on children and the reasons why.
Group discussion. Although they might not realize it or want to admit it, some parents value their children because of their talents, achievements or appearance. Discuss how and why this may happen, and then probe for a deeper basis for the value of children as people made in the image of God and greatly loved by him—loved as they are, not as "potential adults" but as children.
Question 1. If needed, you could follow-up by asking, "What makes them so special to him?"

Jesus is said to be indignant at the disciples for their attitude and actions toward the children. This certainly indicated a reaction of anger, scorn and contempt by the disciples. Later in the passage when the text says Jesus took them in his arms and blessed them, the Greek word there indicates he "blesses them fervently, again and again." The children may have been in the house referred to in verse 10 and were brought to Jesus for a blessing before going to bed. In any event, this stresses Jesus' fervent love for children

(Donald Guthrie, J. Alec Motyer, Alan M. Stibbs and Donald J. Wiseman, eds., *The New Bible Commentary* [Leicester: Inter-Varsity Press 1970], p. 872).

Question 2. Throughout our society, we say we value and cherish our children very highly. Probe for any attitudes and circumstances in society that belie that profession, such as the easy availability of abortions, frequency of divorce (which has been shown to have negative effects on children), the pervasive coarseness and vulgarity to which children are exposed, etc.

Question 6. It's likely that the disciples shared a common view of children still prevalent today: that spending time and energy on children is not nearly as important as with adults. "Jesus is a busy man. He doesn't have time for children. He has important work to do." These attitudes may still prevail among adults in churches today. Ask how these attitudes show themselves in churches and families.

Question 7. The group's answers to questions 3 and 6 will be especially relevant here. You may note the example of Martin Luther who had great difficulty feeling loved by God because he had a cold, distant and harsh father. (Group participants interested in knowing more on this aspect of Luther should read *Here I Stand: A Life of Martin Luther* by Roland H. Bainton [New York: Penguin Books, 1995].)

Question 8. Try to avoid spending a lot of time on discussions of how much a child can understand about Jesus or when a child is "accountable" to God. Keep the discussion focused by reminding participants that Jesus clearly implied that children could receive the kingdom and that, in fact, their natural receptivity and dependence was to be a model for adults.

Question 10. Ask the group how they treat other people and tasks that are high priority for them. How do they treat their children so as to make them a high priority? Try to have parents give you practical examples of making their children a priority, such as scheduling a weekly "date" with children, trying to listen to them carefully and so on.

Question 11. Parents may be accustomed to thinking of themselves as the "teachers" and their children as the "taught," not vice versa. Allow plenty of time for them to think about this question and seek specific examples of how they, as parents, have been taught by their children. Examples might be seeing their quick, unquestioning faith, seeing how children accept the supernatural easily, their colorblindness in racial matters, their compassion and so on.

Study 2. A Firm Family Foundation. Ecclesiastes 4:9-12.
Purpose: To discover some major benefits of a strong, stable marriage, some practical ways to have such a relationship and some major threats to it.

General note. I chose this passage to study rather than more familiar "marriage" passages, such as Ephesians 5:21-33, precisely because such passages are often already very familiar to many groups. A less familiar passage such as this one may not only spark fresher and more lively discussion but introduce participants to a portion of the Bible with which they may be largely unfamiliar. If you'd like to do a more comprehensive study on marriage, you can refer to another LifeGuide: *Marriage: God's Design for Intimacy* by James and Martha Reapsome (Downers Grove, Ill.: InterVarsity Press, 1999).

Question 1. In his new translation and interpretive paraphrase of Ecclesiastes, T. M. Moore paraphrases verse 9 this way: "It seems to me that two who work together and share their lives together do much better than one all alone. For thus we learn to care for others and to trust and love, though this does not come easily" (*Ecclesiastes: Ancient Wisdom When All Else Fails* [Downers Grove, Ill.: InterVarsity Press, 2001], p. 39). He also observes that, "These verses have a common theme: it is dangerous and unwise for the individual to attempt to face life alone, and simple common sense to see the cooperation of others in all that one does" (p. 126).

Also, of course, God observed in creating humans that "it is not good for the man to be alone," so he made a mate for him (Gen 2:18).

Question 2. Some might see here a reference to the presence of Christ (the "third strand") in the marriage, strengthening it immeasurably. Again, T. M. Moore offers this paraphrase of verse 12: "While two can make defense when an assailant comes, one alone will not prevail. If he had only known a true companion and a friend to aid him, he might not have fallen" (p. 39). He comments that the grammatical construction "appears to add faithful friendships to the benefit of a happy marriage" (p. 126). Couples who work at developing strong friendships with other couples have another resource to draw on to help in difficult times.

Question 5. Look to elicit some practical ways spouses can help each other when one "falls" in some way (is sick, burdened at work or by circumstances, is tired, loses patience and so on). Note that parents see things from different perspectives (research shows that men and women parent differently), and that adds to the riches of what they give to their children in parenting.

Question 7. You may want to refer briefly to 2 Corinthians 6:14 and Ephesians 5:21-33 to lead participants to discover what the Bible says about this.

Question 8. Discuss the pros and cons of such relationships. It is often helpful for the spouses each to have at least one close friend outside the relationship—someone to share with who can offer a more neutral or detached view (as we observed in question 2). Having another close friend means that one spouse doesn't have to bear all the emotional needs of the relationship. Still, the goal of the marriage is a strong emotional intimacy, and there is the danger that the "close friend" may substitute for or interfere with the emotional intimacy between the spouses. Also, there is, of course, the real danger of a betrayal of the relationship if one spouse is a close friend with someone of the opposite sex.

Question 9. The most obvious are the sexual temptations allowed by this "sexually-liberated" society and the pressures of work and career, which combined with caring for children, leave little time and energy for spouses to use in maintaining and growing their relationships. Spouses need to be aware of the negative influences that might impact their marriage and actively work together to defend against them.

Question 11. This would be a good question to role-play in the group. Ask if there's a couple willing to act as "mentors" to another couple. Let them role-play an informal counseling situation. The way they counsel is not so important for these purposes as the counsel they give. When the brief "counseling session" is done, have the groups discuss what additional advice they would have given.

Now or Later. One of the great gifts we can give to our children in this day of frequent divorce is the model of a strong, happy marriage—how it gets that way, how it works through tough times and how it stays strong. It is good and important both to model such a relationship and to verbalize your commitment to it for the children.

Study 3. Demonstrating God's Love. 1 Corinthians 13:1-8.

Purpose: To discover the nature of godly love and how we can reflect that love to our children.

General note. In the Bible the word *nurture* is used in the sense of a disciplined training, educating and fostering that grows faith in a child (see Eph 6:4).

Question 1. These verses list patience, kindness and a humble spirit that is not jealous or envious (v. 4). God's love is courteous, not rude and not selfish or self-seeking (v. 5). Such a humble, unselfish attitude is also commended to us in Philippians 2:3-4. One way this godly love expresses patience is in not being easily upset or angered, and its kindness and humility is expressed in not keeping a record of wrongs. Those who have a keen sense of their own weaknesses and sinfulness are slower to keep a record of the failures of others, as is implied by Jesus in Matthew 7:3-5. Godly love does not delight in the evil, the sins or the failures of others but, instead, rejoices with the truth

(v. 6). Godly love is forward-looking, hopeful, gracious, trusting and protecting. Above all, it perseveres; it never fails, never gives up, no matter the circumstance or failure (vv. 7-8).

Question 2. You might also have the group discuss ways parents mistakenly think they show love to their children (indulgence, lax supervision, etc.) and the negative effects such "love" can have.

Question 3. Be aware that some people in the group may have had parents whose "love" so deviated from godly love that they feel it shaped them for ill. If so, let them express that and ask them to contrast that experience with others whose parents more accurately reflected God's love or say how they would have done (or are doing) it differently.

Question 4. Refer to verses 2 and 3. Nothing we do has any lasting value or positive impact apart from the motivation of love.

Question 6. Any discussion of discipline can be controversial. Condemning certain methods of discipline is not the point here. Rather, attempt to establish principles that can guide the choice of discipline methods in a way that reflects godly love. For instance, godly love will not discipline out of anger or a simple lack of patience. It will not do so in a way that intentionally humiliates or embarrasses a child (since such is not loving, because "love covers over a multitude of sins" instead of exposing the "sinner" to public humiliation or continually throwing his failure in his face [1 Pet 4:8]). And of course, it really should "hurt me more than it hurts you," as my father used to say. There is no joy or delight in painful discipline. You shouldn't spend a great deal of time discussing discipline as we'll focus on it exclusively in study 6.

Question 9. Be prepared to suggest some hard situations, such as repeated drug use or serious transgressions against others in the family, and discuss one example of how such a situation might be handled in a way that reflects godly love.

Question 10. For many parents, love means doing whatever it takes to make their child popular such as allowing them to go inappropriate places, wear inappropriate clothes, providing "things" instead of time in relationship with them, giving them freedom to make age-inappropriate decisions, applying inordinate pressure to achieve.

Study 4. Training Our Children in God's Ways. Deuteronomy 6:1-9.

Purpose: To see how we can effectively nurture our children's faith through the events and opportunities of daily family life.

Question 1. The "method" Moses recommended is really a common sense approach that has two parts. One is an implied modeling. When God's commandments are on our hearts, they'll show in our lives, and our children will see them and imitate us. Children are great imitators. Many parents have had (the often disturbing!) experience of hearing their child say to another child the words the parent spoke to them—and in the same tone of voice!

The second part of Moses' approach is to use the everyday, natural occurrences and circumstances of daily family life to help children see and appreciate God's presence and care, as well as learn to practice his ways. It might be likened to "practicing the presence of God" in everyday life, a spiritual approach described in the little book *Practicing the Presence of God* by Brother Lawrence.

Question 4. At that time, most people (other than scribes and priests) were illiterate. They gathered on special occasions to hear God's Word read to them (see, for example, Exodus 24; Nehemiah 8; 2 Chronicles 34). That fact, together with the understanding that children learn best from lessons taught in the midst of daily family life, is likely the reason behind Moses' approach. Today, in our literate society, we can offer our children both the opportunity to hear and read God's Word as well as to learn its lessons in the midst of daily life.

Question 5. Just as a shortbread mold leaves an unalterable impression when pressed on dough, parents can leave a lifelong impression on the lives of their children by the combined force of their example and teaching in the home. This was also Jesus' method with his disciples; verbal teaching as they also lived together and observed and participated in his life and ministry. This is discipling, and that is what Moses urges parents to do for their children: to disciple them. Group participants will likely find helpful the related discussion of parenting styles in Jack and Judith Balswick, *The Family: A Christian Perspective on the Contemporary Home* (Grand Rapids, Mich.: Baker Books, 1999), pp. 108-21.

Question 7. When people in the family are sick, the family can pray for them (and give thanks when they recover). This simple practice teaches that God can be relied on to care for us, that he hears and answers prayer, and that he deserves our thanks. When someone has a test at school or a challenge at work, the family can pray together. When you hear an ambulance or see an accident, pray. When someone in the family experiences a pleasant surprise or blessing, stop and thank God. Pray with your children before big decisions. Say a blessing to each other as you leave in the morning. These are just a few examples to get you started. The discussion can produce many more.

Question 8. It should be clear to the group that "do what I say, not what I do" doesn't work with children. We can't share what we don't have or lead someone somewhere we aren't going ourselves. A good rule for parents to follow is "I will *be* the person I want my child(ren) to *become.*"

Question 9. It's important that our children see us reading and meditating on God's Word regularly if they are to believe us when we say it's "the most important book in the world." They need to see and hear us pray, hear us talking about our faith and our struggles, and hear how God's Word and ways help us. For some, such verbalizing may be new or be somewhat uncomfortable, but it is an important teaching tool.

Question 10. Part of the atmosphere in the home is created by the presence of pictures (of many different kinds) and music. Pictures portraying subjects that show people in acts of faith or that represent God's loving care, together with music that is worshipful and celebrates God's goodness can also foster and strengthen a child's faith.

Question 11. By now, it should be clear that, as helpful as Sunday school, Vacation Bible School (VBS) and youth groups are, they are secondary tools in nurturing faith in our children (and it should be obvious that dropping children off at church without attending oneself is far down on the effectiveness scale). One or two hours a week can't normally overcome what goes on in the home the rest of the week. However, in addition to systematic teaching, Sunday school and regular church attendance do offer the benefit of providing children with different models of faith from the larger faith community. And every parent knows that sometimes children do listen more carefully when someone other than a parent is speaking!

Study 5. The Seasons of Parenting. Ecclesiastes 3:1-8.

Purpose: To see how God provides the time and seasons for the things that are really important in life.

Question 2. This passage would seem to indicate that there is a proper time or season for such things as family projects and common pursuits (vv. 3, 5), family fun (v. 4), celebrations and rituals—both happy and sad—(vv. 4-6), and for just being together and enjoying family love. Your group can probably think of other such activities suggested by this passage also.

T. M. Moore, in his book *Ecclesiastes*, translates verse 1, "There is an appointed time for everything and every matter has its place under the heavens" (p. 31). He says that the message here is that everything has its place in God's plan, even though we can't expect to understand it all completely (p. 123). I take from this passage the assurance that there is a good place in God's plan for activities such as fun, celebrations and other pursuits that strengthen families.

Question 5. Often, parents think they are too busy to "waste" time on fun, but family fun is an important element in building strong families and emotionally healthy children. You might ask people for a particularly vivid and pleasant childhood memory from their family life. Many times it has to do with family fun. Fun family experiences build memories that bind families together during stressful times. They model for children a balanced life of work and play, and they build self-esteem in children when they discover that "Mom and Dad really like me; I'm a fun person."

Question 6. For example, there is the "pre-school season," a time-intensive period of careful, continuing training of young children (a "time to build," v. 3). This is followed by the "elementary-school season" when children are more independent and need our physical presence less but still require much teaching and training (a "time to gather stones," v. 5). The "adolescent/ puberty season" is a challenging time as bodies change and children begin to separate from their parents and attach more to peer groups (a "time to tear and a time to mend," v. 7). The "mid-late teen season" is one of managing the growing independence of children and becoming more of a "coach" than a "trainer" or "director" as in earlier years. This is a time of doing more listening and choosing words carefully (a "time to be silent and a time to speak," v. 7). Verse 6 speaks of a "time to give up"; Moore translates that as "a time for letting lost things go" (p. 31). Each parenting stage is a time of further "letting go," of the dependence of our children on us, and in turn, fostering their growing and healthy independence.

I have given the parenting seasons names from these verses. Perhaps your group would want to choose others. Still, each season has its own particular demands on a parent's time and energy. In each, certain goals and priorities are or are not realistic.

Question 7. Your goal here is to help parents think about whether their goals and priorities for the particular parenting season they are in match the possibilities and demands of that season. Are they realistic? Possible?

Question 8. In addition to recognizing the value of occasional quiet and silence in a noisy world, Moore paraphrases part of verse 7 to say that "sometime keeping quiet shows the wiser path" (p. 32). When is that the case for parents?

Question 10. To begin, you might want to review the "seasons" given in question 6 above or the seasons as named by the group. This is an opinion question, so don't indicate approval or disapproval of any contributions. But if the following are not mentioned (or given much attention), you'll want to suggest "a time to build" (refer to study 3), a time to laugh and to dance (see question 5), and a time to embrace and to love. Everyone, both parents and children, need both physical and verbal expressions of love every day!

Question 11. You might want to read Psalm 31:14-15 to reinforce this point.

Study 6. Godly Discipline in the Home. Hebrews 12:5-11.

Purpose: To discern the motivation and purposes of God's discipline of his children and, from them, to develop and apply guidelines for parental discipline. This will also introduce a positive perspective on discipline.

General note. This will be a controversial discussion throughout. Be prepared! The overall goal or approach to discipline to arrive at by the end of the session is that godly discipline in the home aims ultimately to disciple children; to train them in godly living so they can grow up to be responsible, self-disciplined Christian adults. Discipline is not to be confused with punishment. Discipline, as used in the Bible, has a positive, corrective and restorative motivation and goal; punishment is essentially negative. At the appropriate time, you may introduce the idea that discipline and discipling come from the same Latin root. In a sense, discipline is closely related to discipling.

Group discussion. If people are slow to start the discussion, you can ask them to react to this definition of discipline: "Good discipline is teaching children what to do and punishing them when they don't." This is not the time to be judgmental. Simply accept everyone's contributions, and then move on.

Question 2. God's motivation is clearly a pure and holy love; it is not anger, frustration or a desire to "show them who's the boss." Someone has said that the goal of discipline is to "win children over, not to win over children." There is no "power play" in God's discipline, only the loving desire to "win us over" to a godly life in relationship to him.

Question 3. By now, the group should begin to verbalize the reasons for discipline in positive "discipling language," such as "training them in righteousness" (2 Tim 3:16), "helping them learn how to live as Christians" or "teaching them how to be self-disciplined." You may gently rephrase some suggested reasons into a positive perspective also.

Question 4. People often have strong feelings about discipline, based on how they were disciplined as a child. Be aware that for some this may be a very painful question.

Question 5. My answer is "Yes, probably so." Scripture doesn't skirt the fact that discipline usually is unpleasant for both the disciple (the one being disciplined) and the discipler (parent). Negative consequences are not only effective but also often accurately mirror the way the world works. But again, discipline is not the same as punishment. Although sometimes the methods may be the same, "aversive consequences" are most effective when employed "in the context of a warm, engaged and rational parent-child relationship"; in other words, the parent-child relationship is the key to how negative consequences are received by the child and how effective they are in achieving the goal of producing godly behavior (Balswick and Balswick, *Family*, p. 106).

Question 6. Stress again the link between "discipline" and "discipling." Discipline is *not* the same as punishment. Parents disciple or train their children in godly living with the same motivation that God has in disciplining us: the loving goal that we may grow in godliness and holiness and become "self-disciplined" adult disciples of Christ.

Question 7. Again, this may lead to a somewhat heated discussion. Any discipline methods that are not motivated by love or that don't reflect love or are not likely to contribute to the goal of training disciples would be ruled out by this passage. That includes any methods of discipline that intentionally humiliate or embarrass a child (since such treatment is not loving).

There will inevitably be discussion of spanking. You need to recognize its importance to those who raise it without letting it become the focus of the rest of the group time. A helpful comment may be to note that spanking is often defended on the basis of Proverbs 13:24: "He who spares the rod hates his son." However, in the pastoral culture of Old Testament times, "the rod" was used "to guide ignorant sheep, not (as) a means of beating them into submission" (Balswick and Balswick, *Family*, p. 106). (See the quote from the Balswicks in the note for question 5 also.) The Balswicks, both of whom are professors in the field of marriage and family at Fuller Seminary, note "disciplining children takes time, patience and wisdom. Parents who employ corporal punishment as the primary method of discipline are, by their very behavior, admitting bankruptcy in disciplinary approaches. They are demonstrating an inability to be creative and effective in their discipline of children" (p. 107). Remember, discipline is based on discipling. What methods of discipline best lead to discipling our children?

Question 8. Children need limits and boundaries. The world is too big and a scary place without them. (That's one reason they always seem to be "pushing the limits"; they want to know where the limits are!) They need to know that someone bigger and more competent than they are and who knows what is best is "in charge" to take care of them and to teach them how to live. That is a parent's "job" and responsibility to their children. That's also very encouraging to a child.

Question 10. Godly discipline—discipline that reflects God's loving purposes—is motivated by love, encourages and builds up the child, and is aimed at discipling children to become godly, self-disciplined adults. Your group may add others also.

Question 12. One key to discipling is to remember that it involves both teaching by words and by example. That was Jesus' method of making disciples, and it is still the most effective method of discipling today—especially for children. They're great imitators. They readily (sometimes too readily) absorb and adopt the attitudes of their parents. Effective discipline and discipling begins, therefore, with the parent. Remember the rule from study 4: "I will *be* the person I want my child(ren) to *become.*" Live as a responsible, self-disciplined Christian before your children and that, together with your verbal teaching, will be a powerful discipline tool. This is the "Instrumental Parenting Style" the Balswicks describe as high in both content (teaching) and action (modeling). They rightly call it the "discipling" parenting style, "a system of giving *positive* guidance to children" (pp. 109-10, emphasis added).

Study 7. God Through Our Children's Eyes. Psalm 145.
Purpose: To discover the characteristics of God, especially as they relate to the way God "parents" us and to see how we can apply and reflect those same characteristics in our parenting.

Question 3. Here are a few of the major characteristics of God given in this psalm (and the verses in which they occur) that especially apply to parents: great and worthy of praise (v. 3); good and righteous (v. 7); compassionate (v. 9); faithful to his promises (v. 13); righteous (v. 17); loving (vv. 13, 17); fulfills the desires of his people (v. 19); watches over his people (v. 20). Notice that the characteristics listed refer both to conduct (righteous, faithful, fulfills, watches) as well as moral character (good, compassionate, loving, great). Parents who reflect the character of God in their parenting must reflect both kinds of characteristics.

Question 6. Child development experts agree that our first and strongest impressions of God are derived from our relationship with our parents, especially our father (since we commonly refer to God as our "heavenly father"). But as we grow in our relationship to God and experience him as a good and gracious parent, it also shapes our own parenting. As I experienced a fierce, yet tender, love for my children, I understood something of God's love for me and his sorrow and disappointment at my failures. I understood something of how he feels and reacts to me and my behavior, and that has inevitably shaped how I have related to my own children. As I saw God graciously give me the desires of my heart, I wanted to do that for my children. As I experienced God as so often saying "yes" to me, I wanted to do that, whenever possible, for my children.

Question 7. God is compassionate in setting limits ("commandments"). The loving purpose of the limits shows his compassion: to help us avoid the terrible consequences of ignorance and sin in trying to live outside the boundaries he has set for us. He wants us to live the most joyful, fulfilling life possible in relationship to him, so he sets the limits by which we can do that. That is love and compassion at its most perfect. In addition, God does often show mercy and compassion in sparing us the just consequences of our sin and willfulness.

Question 9. A parent's "job" is to protect, care for and guide their children as they grow. That inevitably means making hard decisions that children will, from time to time, neither understand nor appreciate. But if parents don't do that for their children, who will? Children don't need their parents to be their friends (and that is not the responsibility God has given them); they need them to be their parents. As children grow, they inevitably want more freedom and responsibility than parents want to give them. So parents should not always expect to be appreciated (and will even feel unloved). But that's part of faithful parenting. God has had the same experience with us, his children, so we shouldn't expect it to be any different for us with ours.

Question 11. This is a deeply personal question so responses will likely be varied. Because children take their deepest, most lasting impressions of God from their relationships with their parents, we have a frightening but wonderful opportunity. In our marriage as well, we can show our children something of the faithful, covenant love of God. We'll also have plenty of opportunities to show his grace and mercy. In all relationships (including with people outside the home) we can show his compassion. Daily, we can show his loving delight in his children. The group will undoubtedly come up with others. Certainly, we'll have plenty of opportunities to show most of the characteristics we listed in the note to question 3.

Study 8. Coping with the "Lost" Child. Luke 15:11-32.

Purpose: To offer help and encouragement to parents whose children have strayed from or rejected the faith and gone "to a far country."

Group discussion. If there are parents in the group with "lost" children, it is important that the group be sensitive, not judgmental, and let the parents share details or feelings only to the extent that they are comfortable doing so.

Question 1. This is largely speculation, but his motivation may have grown out of youthful immaturity. The text can be read to imply that his motivation was a youthful desire to "see the world" (a "distant country," v. 13) or a desire to have greater independence.

Question 2. Verse 20 certainly implies he was watching and waiting, no doubt hoping for his son to return. This does not rule out feelings of disappointment, anxiety or even anger, however.

Question 5. The father's love here is unfailing and unconditional. Interpreters generally agree that Jesus told this story (and the two parables that immediately precede it in this chapter) in order to illustrate God's unfailing, pardoning love for the lost and how he rejoices at their return. For example, see Leon Morris, *The Gospel According to St. Luke,* Tyndale New Testament Commentaries (Grand Rapids, Mich.: Eerdmans, 1979), pp. 239-40.

Question 7. It is clear that he was a self-righteous young man who did not share his father's pardoning love.

Question 8. Again, this can be a very sensitive question depending on the depth of hurt, disappointment and anger a parent feels. Give room for a wide expression of opinions and trust that, as the group moves through the study, God's attitude toward repentant sinners will become clear.

Question 9. The son clearly recognized his sin, confessed it (v. 21) and accepted responsibility for it. He knew he had fractured family relationships and thus he returned to his father in a spirit of repentance, sorrow and humility (vv. 18-19, 21). The father maintained a spirit of unfailing, forgiving love, compassion (v. 20) and hope (he was watching and waiting for his son to come home). His loving, compassionate spirit must have made it easier for his son to return home with some confidence that his father would receive him and grant his request. Morris notes the "overflowing joy" of the father at his son's return, evidenced in the celebration that followed (Morris, *Gospel According to St. Luke,* pp. 242-43).

Question 10. The return of a lost child may require, of both the child and parent, the attitudes and actions described in this parable. The "conditions" of such a return may reflect these attitudes and actions. There may well be a need to see that such a child accepts responsibility for their actions by seeking professional help and reestablishing trust in some way. Nothing, however, should overshadow the unfailing, pardoning love for the repentant sinner also at the heart of this parable.

Questions 11-12. Many parents feel deep guilt over children who have strayed. They may be keenly aware of some responsibility they share for that. In the end, however, children grow up and make their own choices. They are not computers that parents can "program." Our children make their own choices and bear their own responsibility for them.

Question 13. The good news of this parable is that lost children do return, especially when they know that a parent's unfailing, pardoning love is ready to receive them. There are no guarantees in parenting except that God is faithful. He hears and answers prayer and, as this parable is meant to show, rejoices at the return of one who is lost. Parents, armed with unfailing love and who are faithful in prayer, can hope for and expect their lost child to return, even as did the father in this parable.

Question 14. This is a very difficult question for a parent of a lost child. I suggest saying something like, "She hasn't 'turned out' yet. God isn't finished with her. But then, he's not finished with me, and I haven't turned out yet either."

Study 9. Creating a Legacy for Our Children. Joshua 4:1-9, 19-24.

Purpose: To recognize the importance of building a spiritual legacy for our children, learn what such a legacy could be and see how to begin to build it.

Group discussion. Some in the group (those physically or emotionally abused, or children of alcoholics or of divorce, for example) may have received primarily negative "legacies" from their parents. They should be encouraged to discuss the negatives (if they are comfortable doing so) and talk about what they've learned and how they would want to do things differently in their own parenting. This can help provide a positive perspective to an otherwise painful, uncomfortable group experience.

Personal reflection. Acknowledge that some may have received primarily negative legacies and encourage reflection along the lines suggested above.

Question 2. The stones were more than just a reminder of the specific act at the Jordan but were tied to the larger reminder that God had acted on their behalf numerous times in the past. He is a caring, powerful God who, it is implied, could be counted on to also act on their behalf in the future. In the end, God would be glorified among all people who heard of these great works, even for generations to come.

Question 6. It is significant to remember that the spiritual legacy we build for our children also influences the spiritual lives of our grandchildren and quite possibly generations beyond. It can, through those who follow after us, have an impact and witness to the wider world around them.

Questions 8-9. Discuss the tangible "reminders," habits, practices and spiritual disciplines that parents can develop in the family during the parenting years. In this age of "disposable relationships," the legacy and example of a strong, lasting marriage is also a great gift to our children.

Question 10. The hardest part may be just making the effort and taking the time in the midst of busy daily lives. Or people may feel "unqualified," not "spiritual" enough. But we find the time to do the really important things, our high priorities. In a few minutes together, a couple can review the two or three highest priority "stones" they want to use to build a legacy and then discuss how to start. It doesn't have to happen all in one day! As for being "super-spiritual," most Israelite parents were "ordinary folks" just like us.

Question 11. There are many ways to build a lasting spiritual legacy for our children, and each parent or parents will choose to focus on one or two that fit best with their goals and personalities. There's no single "right answer" here. But the greatest impact we have on our children is through who we are. Our children see how we live and relate to God, our family and others. When we grow our personal relationship with God, it inevitably strengthens our marriage and has a positive impact on our children. Again, resolve to *"be the person you want your child(ren) to become."*

Now or Later. Encourage parents to identify a time in the week ahead to discuss the spiritual legacy they want to build for their children and two or three ways to begin (or continue) to build it. Encourage them to meet perhaps two or three times in the year ahead with one or two other couples to share ideas, to pray and to encourage each other in this challenging task.

You may also suggest that participants look at the stories of Daniel (1:8-17; 6:6-23), Samuel (1 Samuel 1:11, 26-28), Joseph (Genesis 39:1-21), Moses (Hebrews 11:23-29) and Timothy (2 Timothy 1:3-5) as examples of children who were left a spiritual legacy that had a clear, positive life impact.

Richard Patterson Jr. is vice president of editorial services at Scripture Union/ USA. He previously served Scripture Union as children and family ministry specialist (1988-2001) and as vice president of field ministry (2001-2004). His books include Brand Name Kids; It's the Little Things That Count *and* Confident Parenting in Challenging Times. *He lives in Clifton Park, New York. He can be contacted through his website <www.confidentparenting.com>.*

What Should We Study Next?

A good place to continue your study of Scripture would be with a book study. Many groups begin with a Gospel such as *Mark* (20 studies by Jim Hoover) or *John* (26 studies by Douglas Connelly). These guides are divided into two parts so that if twenty or twenty-six weeks seems like too much to do at once, the group can feel free to do half and take a break with another topic. Later you might want to come back to it. You might prefer to try a shorter letter. *Philippians* (9 studies by Donald Baker), *Ephesians* (11 studies by Andrew T. and Phyllis J. Le Peau) and *1 & 2 Timothy and Titus* (11 studies by Pete Sommer) are good options. If you want to vary your reading with an Old Testament book, consider *Ecclesiastes* (12 studies by Bill and Teresa Syrios) for a challenging and exciting study.

There are a number of interesting topical LifeGuide studies as well. Here are some options for filling three or four quarters of a year:

Basic Discipleship
Christian Beliefs, 12 studies by Stephen D. Eyre
Christian Character, 12 studies by Andrea Sterk & Peter Scazzero
Christian Disciplines, 12 studies by Andrea Sterk & Peter Scazzero
Evangelism, 12 studies by Rebecca Pippert & Ruth Siemens

Building Community
Fruit of the Spirit, 9 studies by Hazel Offner
Spiritual Gifts, 8 studies by R. Paul Stevens
Christian Community, 10 studies by Rob Suggs

Character Studies
David, 12 studies by Jack Kuhatschek
New Testament Characters, 10 studies by Carolyn Nystrom
Old Testament Characters, 12 studies by Peter Scazzero
Women of the Old Testament, 12 studies by Gladys Hunt

The Trinity
Meeting God, 12 studies by J. I. Packer
Meeting Jesus, 13 studies by Leighton Ford
Meeting the Spirit, 10 studies by Douglas Connelly